Math Counts

Weight

Introduction

In keeping with the major goals of the National Council of Teachers of Mathematics Curriculum and Evaluation Standards, children will become mathematical problem solvers, learn to communicate mathematically, and learn to reason mathematically by using the series Math Counts.

Pattern, Shape, and *Size* may be investigated first—in any sequence.

Sorting, Counting, and *Numbers* may be used next, followed by *Time, Length, Weight,* and *Capacity.*

Ramona G. Choos, Professor of Mathematics, Senior Adviser to the Dean of Continuing Education, Chicago State University; Sponsor for Chicago Elementary Teachers' Mathematics Club

About this Book

Mathematics is a part of a child's world. It is not only interpreting numbers or mastering tricks of addition or multiplication. Mathematics is about *ideas*. These ideas have been developed to explain particular qualities such as size, weight, and height, as well as relationships and comparisons. Yet all too often the important part that an understanding of mathematics will play in a child's development is forgotten or ignored.

Most adults can solve simple mathematical tasks without the need for counters, beads, or fingers. Young children find such abstractions almost impossible to master. They need to see, talk, touch, and experiment.

The photographs and text in these books have been chosen to encourage talk about topics that are essentially mathematical. By talking, the young reader can explore some of the central concepts that support mathematics. It is on an understanding of these concepts that a child's future mastery of mathematics will be built.

Henry Pluckrose

1995 Childrens Press® Edition
© 1994 Watts Books, London, New York, Sydney
All rights reserved.
Printed in the United States of America.
Published simultaneously in Canada.
3 4 5 6 7 8 9 0 R 04 03 02 01 00 99 98

Math Counts

Weight

By Henry Pluckrose

Mathematics Consultant: Ramona G. Choos,
Professor of Mathematics

 CHILDRENS PRESS®
CHICAGO

Weight is a measuring word.
We weigh things to find out
how heavy they are.

4

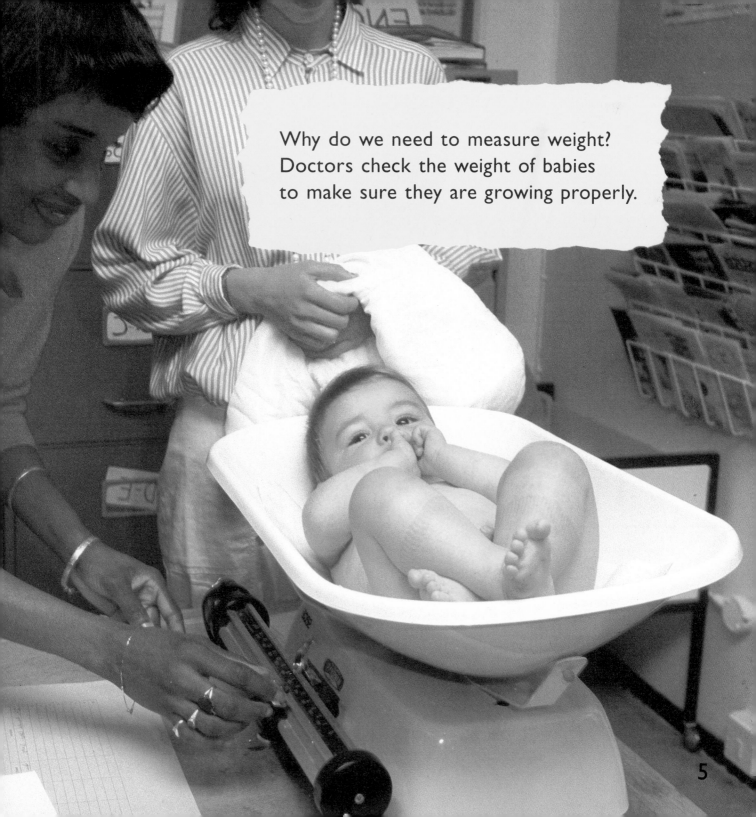

Why do we need to measure weight? Doctors check the weight of babies to make sure they are growing properly.

5

We weigh ingredients when we cook.
Only a small quantity of flour
is needed to make a cake.
We weigh small quantities in grams or ounces.

This flour is being weighed
before it is sent to the bakery.
Large quantities of flour
are needed to make
all the bread
sold in a supermarket.
Large quantities are weighed
in kilograms or pounds.

7

Everything weighs something,
even very light things
like letters or postcards.

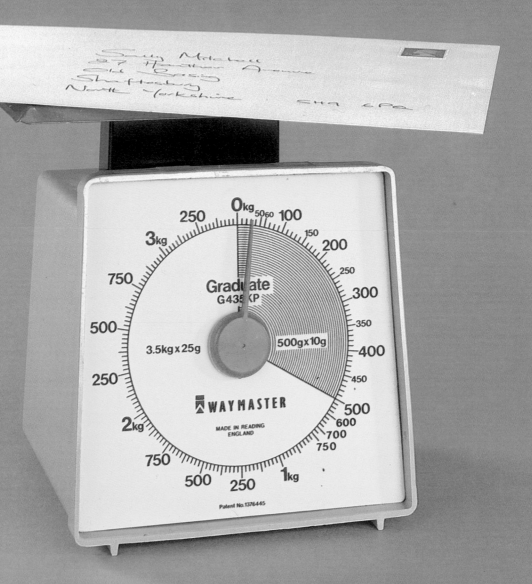

There are lots of letters
and postcards
in these mailbags.
Why are the bags so heavy?

9

Sometimes we can guess
the weight of things.
Which do you think is lighter,
the feather or the stone?

How would you make sure
that you have guessed correctly?

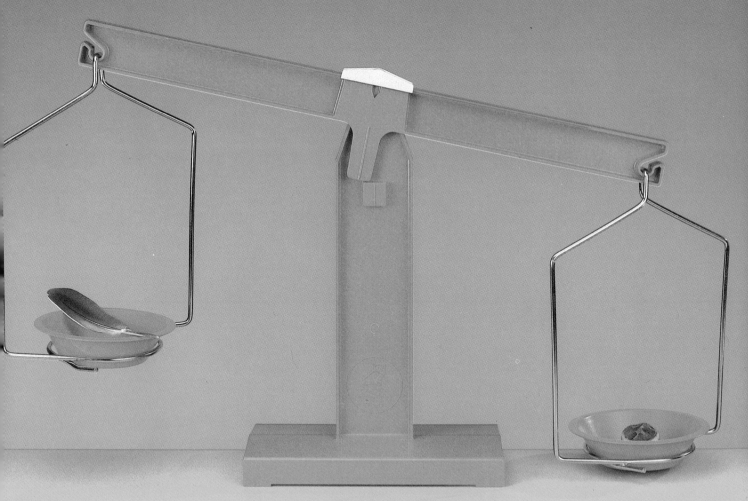

Guessing that one thing is heavier than another is not always easy.

How will you find out for sure
which pile of tea is heavier?

You could put a stone in one pan of this scale.
Which is heavier—the tea bags

or the tea?
How do you know?

But stones come in different weights.
So we use standard weights to measure heaviness.
Many countries use the metric system to measure heaviness.
1000 grams make one kilogram.

A kilogram of apples weighs
exactly the same
wherever you buy it.

If the apples were heavier than a kilogram the scales would not balance.

If the apples were lighter than a kilogram the scales would not balance either.

You can use scales to compare the weight of different things. A kilogram of apples is as heavy as a kilogram of potatoes.

Would a kilogram of rice
weigh more, less, or the same
as a kilogram of cheese?

It is important to know
how heavy things are.
Clerks often weigh food
when they sell it.
We pay for the weight of food
that we buy.

22

Even when food is sold in packages,
the weight of the contents
is marked on the label.

Luggage is weighed at the airport before it is loaded onto a plane.

24

If a plane were overloaded it could not fly safely.

25

Trucks and vans must not be overloaded either.
This small truck could not carry

something as heavy as this.

Crane operators have to be sure that the crane is strong enough to lift the weight of the goods it is moving.

Notices next to some bridges tell drivers
the weight that the bridges can carry.
Very heavy trucks cannot travel
over this bridge.
The bridge would not support
their weight.

Some people lift heavy weights as a sport.

How heavy were
you when you were
last weighed?
Are you heavier now?

Library of Congress Cataloging-in-Publication Data

Pluckrose, Henry Arthur.
    weight / Henry Pluckrose.
      p.   cm.
    Originally published: London; New York: F. Watts, 1988.
    (Math counts)
    Includes index.
    Summary: Photographs and text introduce the concept of weight and how to measure it.
    ISBN 0-516-05460-0
    1. Weights and measures — Juvenile literature. [1. Weights and measures.] I. Title.
QC90.6.P58   1995
530.8 — dc20   94-38010
                                                                       CIP
                                                                        AC

Photographic credits: Chris Fairclough, 4, 5, 6, 7, 8, 10, 11, 12, 13, 14, 15, 16, 17, 18, 19, 20, 21, 23, 24, 26, 28, 29; PhotoEdit © Michael Newman, 9, 22, 31; Unicorn Stock Photos © Aneal Vohra, 25; Quadrant Picture Library, 27; ZEFA, 30

Editor: Ruth Thomson
Assistant Editor: Annabel Martin
Design: Chloë Cheesman

INDEX